My Very First OXFORD Dictionary

D0519947

My name is

'For Rose, Amy and Eleanor' — C.K.

OXFORD
UNIVERSITY PRESS

Great Clarendon Street, Oxford OX2 6DP

Oxford University Press is a department of the University of Oxford.
It furthers the University's objective of excellence in research, scholarship,
and education by publishing worldwide in

Oxford New York

Athens Auckland Bangkok Bogotá Buenos Aires Calcutta
Cape Town Chennai Dar es Salaam Delhi Florence Hong Kong Istanbul
Karachi Kuala Lumpur Madrid Melbourne Mexico City Mumbai
Nairobi Paris São Paulo Singapore Taipei Tokyo Toronto Warsaw

with associated companies in Berlin Ibadan

Oxford is a registered trade mark of Oxford University Press
in the UK and in certain other countries

© Oxford University Press 1999

First published 1999

All rights reserved. No part of this publication may be reproduced, stored in a retrieval system, or
transmitted, in any form or by any means, without the prior permission in writing of Oxford
University Press. Within the UK, exceptions are allowed in respect of any fair dealing for the
purpose of research or private study, or criticism or review, as permitted under the Copyright,
Designs and Patents Act 1988, or in the case of reprographic reproduction in accordance with
the terms of the licences issued by the Copyright Licensing Agency. Enquiries concerning
reproduction outside these terms and in other countries should be sent to the Rights
Department, Oxford University Press, at the address above
This book is sold subject to the condition that it shall not, by way of trade or otherwise, be lent,
re-sold, hired out or otherwise circulated without the publisher's prior consent in any form of
binding or cover other than that in which it is published and without a similar condition
including this condition being imposed on the subsequent purchaser

British Library Cataloguing in Publication Data
Data available

ISBN 0-19-910503-0 (paperback)
ISBN 0-19-910502-2 (hardback)
ISBN 0-19-910562-6 (Big Book)
5–7–9–10–8–6–4

Typeset in Gill Sans Schoolbook
Printed in China

My Very First OXFORD Dictionary

Compiled by Clare Kirtley

Illustrated by Georgie Birkett

OXFORD

UNIVERSITY PRESS

Contents

Introduction

My Very First Oxford Dictionary helps young children enjoy and discover the features of a dictionary. It contains over 300 words in alphabetical order, each with a simple definition and a colourful picture. There are also additional end sections with words that children will find useful when writing. The words have been chosen to support and develop speaking, reading, and writing.

Here are the main features on the **A** to **Z** pages:

alphabet

capital letter

letter

symbol for verb

picture

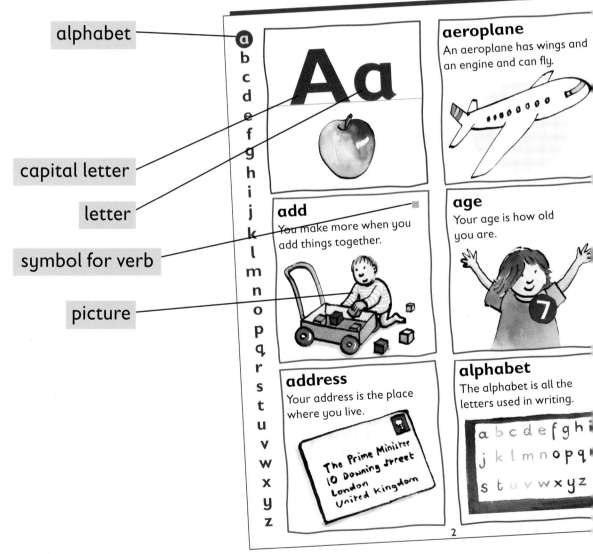

aeroplane
An aeroplane has wings and an engine and can fly.

add
You make more when you add things together.

age
Your age is how old you are.

address
Your address is the place where you live.

The Prime Minister
10 Downing Street
London
United Kingdom

alphabet
The alphabet is all the letters used in writing.

a b c d e f g h i
j k l m n o p q
s t u v w x y z

2

My Very First Oxford Dictionary is an ideal introduction to dictionaries and other alphabetically ordered reference books. It helps children acquire basic dictionary and reference skills in a simple and enjoyable way: they can learn about the alphabet and about alphabetical order; they can find out how to locate a word by using the initial letter; they can check their own spelling; and they can learn how to use simple definitions of words.

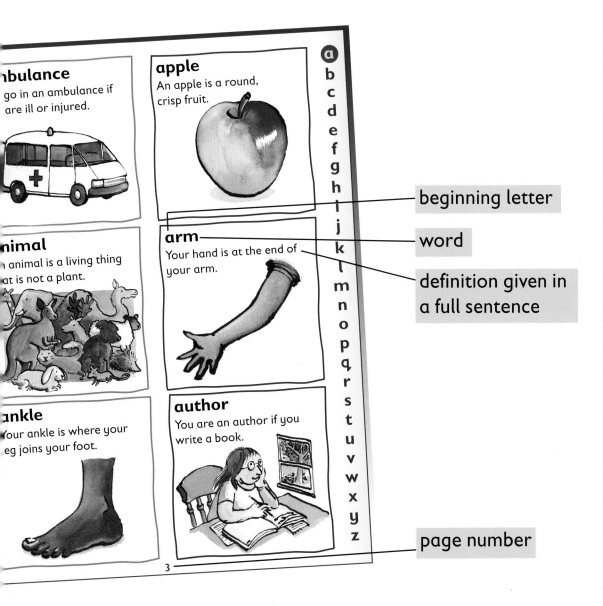

bulance
go in an ambulance if are ill or injured.

apple
An apple is a round, crisp fruit.

nimal
animal is a living thing at is not a plant.

arm
Your hand is at the end of your arm.

ankle
Your ankle is where your leg joins your foot.

author
You are an author if you write a book.

a
b
c
d
e
f
g
h
i
j
k
l
m
n
o
p
q
r
s
t
u
v
w
x
y
z

beginning letter

word

definition given in a full sentence

page number

3

Aa

aeroplane
An aeroplane has wings and an engine and can fly.

add
You make more when you add things together.

age
Your age is how old you are.

address
Your address is the place where you live.

The Prime Minister
10 Downing Street
London
United Kingdom

alphabet
The alphabet is all the letters used in writing.

abcdefghi
jklmnopqr
stuvwxyz

ambulance

You go in an ambulance if you are ill or injured.

apple

An apple is a round, crisp fruit.

animal

An animal is a living thing that is not a plant.

arm

Your hand is at the end of your arm.

ankle

Your ankle is where your leg joins your foot.

author

You are an author if you write a book.

Bb

bear

A bear is a big furry animal.

ball

A ball is round. You can play games with it.

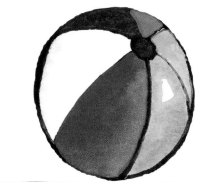

bed

You sleep in a bed.

banana

A banana is a long yellow fruit.

bicycle

A bicycle has two wheels. You ride a bicycle.

big

If something is big it is large.

bounce

A ball comes back up again when you bounce it.

bird

A bird has wings, feathers and a beak.

bread

You make bread with flour and bake it in the oven.

book

A book has pages and a cover.

bus

A bus can carry lots of people.

Cc

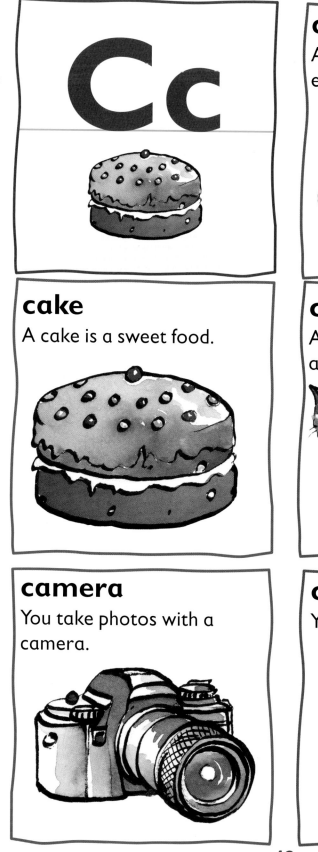

car

A car has wheels and an engine.

cake

A cake is a sweet food.

cat

A cat is a small furry animal.

camera

You take photos with a camera.

chair

You sit on a chair.

cheese
You make cheese from milk.

cook
You cook food by heating it.

clock
A clock tells you the time.

cow
A cow is a farm animal that gives milk.

computer
A computer stores information.

cup
You drink things from a cup.

a b **c** d e f g h i j k l m n o p q r s t u v w x y z

Dd

day

It is light during the day.

dance

You move to music when you dance.

dinosaur

A dinosaur is an animal that lived a long time ago.

date

A date is the day something happens.

MONDAY
5
MARCH

doctor

A doctor makes you better if you are ill.

dog

You can keep a dog as a pet.

dress

A girl sometimes wears a dress.

doll

A doll is a toy person.

drink

You can drink milk.

door

You open a door to go into a room.

duck

A duck is a bird that likes water.

a b c **d** e f g h i j k l m n o p q r s t u v w x y z

Ee

eat

You need to eat food to live.

ear

You use your ears to hear.

egg

A bird lives inside an egg before it is born.

earth

You live on the planet Earth.

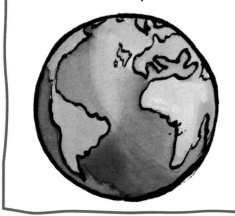

elbow

You bend your arm at your elbow.

electricity

You use electricity to get light and heat.

envelope

You put a letter in an envelope.

elephant

An elephant has a long nose called a trunk.

exercise

You need to exercise to keep fit.

empty

If something is empty it has nothing in it.

eye

You use your eyes to see.

a b c d **e** f g h i j k l m n o p q r s t u v w x y z

Ff

farm

A farm is where food is grown.

fairy

You can read about a fairy in stories.

fall

You come down quickly when you fall.

feather

Birds have feathers instead of fur or hair.

fish

A fish lives under water.

flower

A flower is part of a plant.

fox

A fox is a wild animal with a furry tail.

foot

Your foot is at the end of your leg.

frog

A frog has wet skin and webbed feet.

fork

You use a fork to eat.

fruit

You can eat fruit. Apples and oranges are fruit.

a b c d e **f** g h i j k l m n o p q r s t u v w x y z

Gg

garden

You can grow flowers and vegetables in a garden.

game

You play a game.

gate

A gate is an outside door.

garage

A car is kept in a garage.

giant

A giant is a very big person.

giraffe
A giraffe has a long neck.

good
If something is good you like it.

glass
A window is made of glass.

grow
Things get bigger when they grow.

glue
You use glue to stick things together.

guitar
A guitar is an instrument with strings.

a b c d e f **g** h i j k l m n o p q r s t u v w x y z

Hh

head

Your eyes and ears are on your head.

hand

You hold things with your hand.

helicopter

A helicopter has blades that spin round on top.

hat

You wear a hat on your head.

hill

A hill is a piece of high land.

holiday

A holiday is when you do not go to school or work.

hot

If something is hot it can burn you.

horse

You can ride a horse.

house

You can live in a house.

hospital

You go to hospital if you are ill.

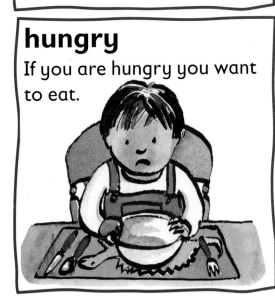

hungry

If you are hungry you want to eat.

a b c d e f g h i j k l m n o p q r s t u v w x y z

Ii

information

You use information to find out about things.

ice

Freezing water turns to ice.

insect

An insect is a small animal with six legs.

ill

If you are ill you do not feel well.

instrument

You use an instrument to make music.

Jj

jug
You use a jug to pour a drink.

jam
You make jam from fruit and sugar.

juggler
A juggler throws things up and catches them.

journey
You travel from place to place on a journey.

jump
You go up into the air when you jump.

a b c d e f g h i **j** k l m n o p q r s t u v w x y z

Kk

kettle

You use a kettle to boil water.

kangaroo

A kangaroo has big back legs and jumps.

key

You use a key to unlock a door.

keep

If you keep something you do not give it away.

kick

You kick a ball with your foot.

kind

You are being kind when you help other people.

kite

A kite flies in the air at the end of a long string.

king

Some countries are ruled by a king.

knee

Your knee is where your leg bends.

kitchen

You cook in a kitchen.

knife

You use a knife to cut things.

a b c d e f g h i j **k** l m n o p q r s t u v w x y z

Ll

leaf

A leaf grows on a plant.

ladybird

A ladybird is a small flying insect with spots.

leg

You use your legs to walk.

laugh

You laugh when something is funny.

letter

You use letters to write words.

and

library

Books are kept in a library.

little

If something is little it is not big.

like

If you like someone you think they are nice.

look

You use your eyes to look.

lion

A lion is a big wild cat.

loud

You can hear loud sounds easily.

a b c d e f g h i j k l m n o p q r s t u v w x y z

29

Mm

meat

We eat meat from animals.

make

You make something by putting things together.

metal

Something made of metal is hard.

map

A map shows you how to get to places.

microwave

A microwave oven cooks food quickly.

30

milk

You can drink cow's milk.

moon

You often see the moon in the sky at night.

money

You use money to buy things.

mountain

A mountain is a high hill.

monkey

A monkey is furry and lives in trees.

mouth

You use your mouth to speak and eat.

a b c d e f g h i j k l **m** n o p q r s t u v w x y z

N n

necklace

You wear a necklace around your neck.

name

Your name is what people call you.

nest

A bird lives in a nest.

neck

Your neck joins your head to your shoulders.

new

Something is new when you first get it.

nice

If something is nice you enjoy it.

nose

You use your nose to smell.

night

It is dark at night time.

number

You use numbers to count.

noise

A noise is a loud sound.

nurse

A nurse looks after you when you are ill.

a b c d e f g h i j k l m **n** o p q r s t u v w x y z

Oo

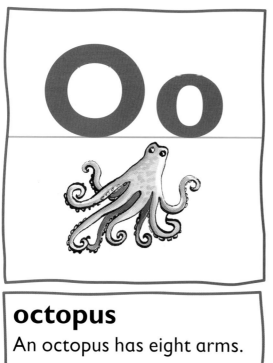

open

You can open a door.

octopus

An octopus has eight arms.

orange

An orange is a round fruit with thick peel.

old

You are old if you were born a long time ago.

owl

An owl is a bird who flies at night.

Pp

park
You can play in a park.

page
A page is part of a book.

pencil
You use a pencil to write or draw.

paper
You write on paper.

piano
A piano is an instrument with black and white keys.

pig
A pig is a fat farm animal.

play
You have fun when you play.

plant
A plant grows out of the ground.

pull
You can pull with your arms.

plate
You put food on a plate.

push
You push a wheelbarrow.

queue

You line up in a queue to wait for a bus.

queen

A queen is a woman who rules a country.

quick

You are quick when you move fast.

question

You ask a question to find out something.

quiet

You are quiet when you make very little noise.

a b c d e f g h i j k l m n o p **q** r s t u v w x y z

Rr

rainbow
Sun shines through rain to make a rainbow.

rabbit
A rabbit is a small animal with long ears.

read
You read books, cards and letters.

rain
The rain is water falling from the sky.

recorder
A recorder is an instrument that you blow.

rhinoceros

A rhinoceros has a horn on its nose.

robot

A robot is a machine that moves like a person.

river

A river is a large stream of water.

rocket

A rocket sends spacecraft into space.

road

Cars and buses travel on a road.

run

You move your legs quickly to run.

a b c d e f g h i j k l m n o p q **r** s t u v w x y z

39

Ss

seed

A plant grows from a seed.

school

You go to school to learn.

sheep

You get wool from a sheep.

scissors

You use scissors to cut things.

shirt

A shirt has sleeves and a collar.

shoe
You wear a shoe on your foot.

sock
You wear a sock on your foot.

shop
You buy things in a shop.

story
A story tells you about something that has happened.

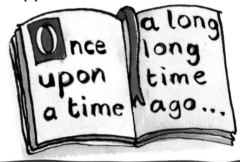

snow
Snow falls when it is very cold.

sun
It is warm and bright in the sun.

Tt

teeth

You use your teeth to bite.

table

You sit at a table.

telephone

You use a telephone to speak to people.

teacher

A teacher helps you to learn.

television

You watch and listen to things on television.

towel

You use a towel to dry yourself.

train

A train goes on a track.

town

There are lots of buildings in a town.

tree

A tree is a tall plant with leaves.

toy

You play with a toy.

trousers

You wear trousers on your legs.

a b c d e f g h i j k l m n o p q r s **t** u v w x y z

Uu

uniform

The police and nurses wear a uniform.

ugly

If something is ugly it is not nice to look at.

upset

You are not happy when you are upset.

umbrella

You use an umbrella to keep dry when it rains.

use

You use tools to make things.

vegetable

A vegetable is a plant that you can eat.

van

A van can carry lots of things.

video

A video records sound and pictures from the television.

vase

You put flowers in a vase.

violin

You play a violin with a bow.

a b c d e f g h i j k l m n o p q r s t u v w x y z

Ww

wind

The wind is air moving.

wall

A wall is made of brick or stone.

word

You use words when you speak or write.

dog
chair
bed
hat

water

Rivers and seas are made up of water.

write

You write words for other people to read.

write
w

Xx

Yy

X-ray
An X-ray shows the inside of your body.

yacht
A yacht is a boat with sails.

xylophone
A xylophone is an instrument with wooden bars.

yawn
You yawn when you are tired.

year

There are twelve months in a year.

Zz

yogurt

You make yogurt from sour milk.

zebra

A zebra has black and white stripes.

young

You are young if you were born a short time ago.

zigzag

A zigzag line turns sharply.

zip

You do some coats up
with a zip.

zoo

You can see wild animals
at a zoo.

a b c d e f g h i j k l m n o p q r s t u v w x y z

49

Words we write a lot

a
about
after
again
all
am
an
and
another
are
as
at
away

back
ball
be
because
bed
been
big
boy
brother
but
by

call
called
came
can
can't
cat
children
come
could
cross

dad
day
did
dig
do
dog
don't
door
down

end
every
everyone

first
for
from

get
girl
go
going
good
got

had
half
has
have
he
help
her
here
him
his
home
house
how

I
if
in
is
it

jump
just

last
laugh
like
liked
little
live
lived
look
looked
lots
love

made
make
man
many
may
me
more
much
mum
must
my

name
new
next
night
no
not
now

said
saw
school
see
seen
she
should
sister
sit
so
some

under
up
us

very

want
was
water
way
we
went
were
what
when
where
who
why
will
with
would

of
off
old
on
once
one
or
our
out
over

people
play
please
pull
pulled
push
put

ran

take
than
thank
that
the
their
them
then
there
these
they
this
three
time
to
too
took
tree
two

yes
you
your

Verbs (These are doing words)

add

bounce

buy

call

carry

catch

clap

climb

cook

cry

cut

dance

dig

drink

grow

keep

eat

hear

kick

exercise

help

laugh

hop

fall

jump

like

More verbs

listen

paint

run

look

play

see

pull

make

push

sing

open

read

sit

sleep

talk

walk

smell

taste

wash

throw

smile

write

write

touch

take

use

yawn

Colours

red

blue

green

yellow

purple

orange

brown

black

grey

white

pink

Shapes

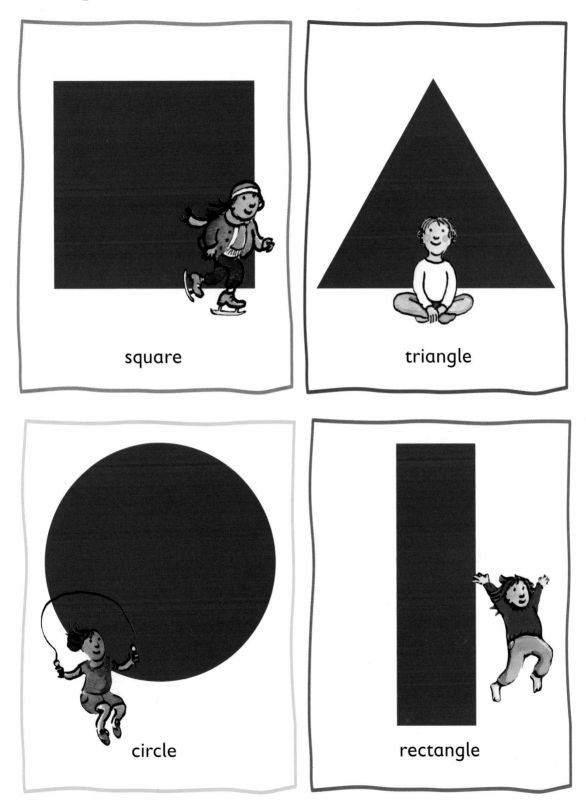

square

triangle

circle

rectangle

Days of the week

Sunday

Monday

Tuesday

Wednesday

Thursday

Friday

Saturday

Months of the year

January

February

March

April

May

June

July

August

September

October

November

December

Numbers

zero	**0**	
one	1	
two	**2**	
three	**3**	
four	4	
five	**5**	
six	**6**	
seven	**7**	
eight	8	
nine	**9**	

ten **10**

eleven **11**

twelve 12

thirteen **13**

fourteen **14**

fifteen 15

sixteen **16**

seventeen **17**

eighteen **18**

nineteen 19

twenty **20**

The alphabet

Aa

Bb

Cc

Dd

Ee

Ff

Gg

Hh

Ii

Jj

Kk

Ll

Mm

Tt

Nn

Uu

Oo

Vv

Pp

Ww

Qq

Xx

Rr

Yy

Ss

Zz